how to draw
CARS &
TRUCKS

Written and Illustrated by **Michael LaPlaca**

Watermill Press

materials

The first things you'll need are some pencils. Number 2 pencils are best. You'll also need some white paper (a pad is good to have), an eraser, crayons, a scissors, a felt-tip pen, construction paper, and glue.

Before you begin:

Here are a few hints on how to draw cars and trucks. The car or truck that you will be drawing is shown at the top of each page. Below it are several easy steps for you to follow. The first step shows the basic shapes that you will use to start your drawing.

Add to your drawing, step by step, until it looks just the way you want it. Take your time as you work, and look at all the details shown in each step. Use pencil as you work. When the pencil sketch is done, erase any unwanted lines. Then go over your drawing with a felt-tip pen. Use crayons to color the finished drawing.

After you've colored your drawing, you might like to carefully cut it out and glue it to a sheet of brightly colored construction paper. You can draw a whole scene. Show roads, trees, houses, or anything you like. Placing several cars and trucks together looks nice, too. Cars and trucks are lots of fun to draw, so have a great time!

Now let's draw cars and trucks.

sedan

A sedan is a car that has a closed top and a front and rear seat. This is a four-door sedan.

1. A sedan is easy to draw. Start with two box shapes.

2. Next, round off the back of the car and shape the roof to look like this. Add the wheels.

3. Add the bumpers, doors, head-, tail-, and sidelights, and you have drawn a sedan.

A coupé (coo-PAY) is a closed car that has only two doors. It often has a more sporty look than a two-door sedan.

coupé

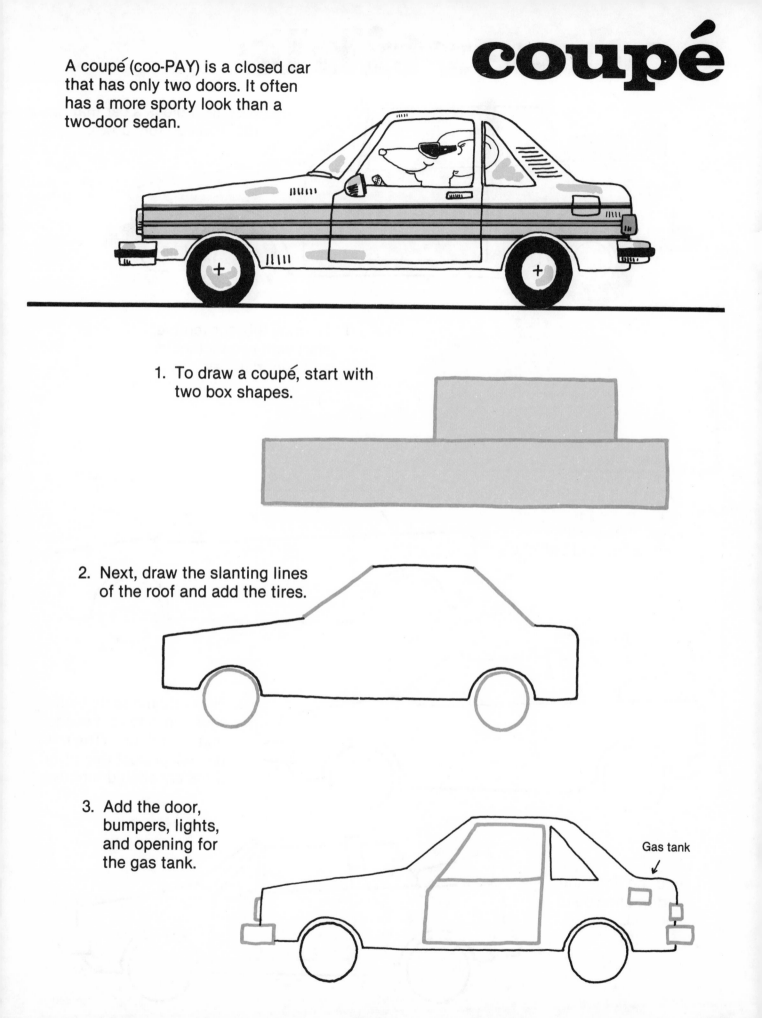

1. To draw a coupé, start with two box shapes.

2. Next, draw the slanting lines of the roof and add the tires.

3. Add the door, bumpers, lights, and opening for the gas tank.

Gas tank

convertible

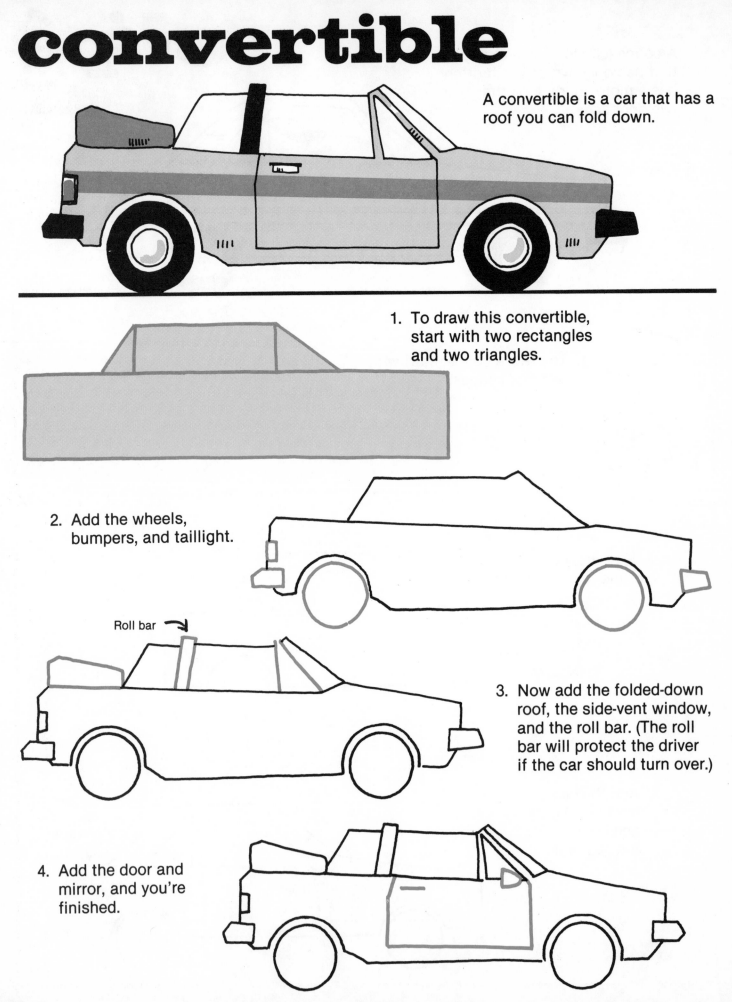

A convertible is a car that has a roof you can fold down.

1. To draw this convertible, start with two rectangles and two triangles.

2. Add the wheels, bumpers, and taillight.

Roll bar

3. Now add the folded-down roof, the side-vent window, and the roll bar. (The roll bar will protect the driver if the car should turn over.)

4. Add the door and mirror, and you're finished.

police car

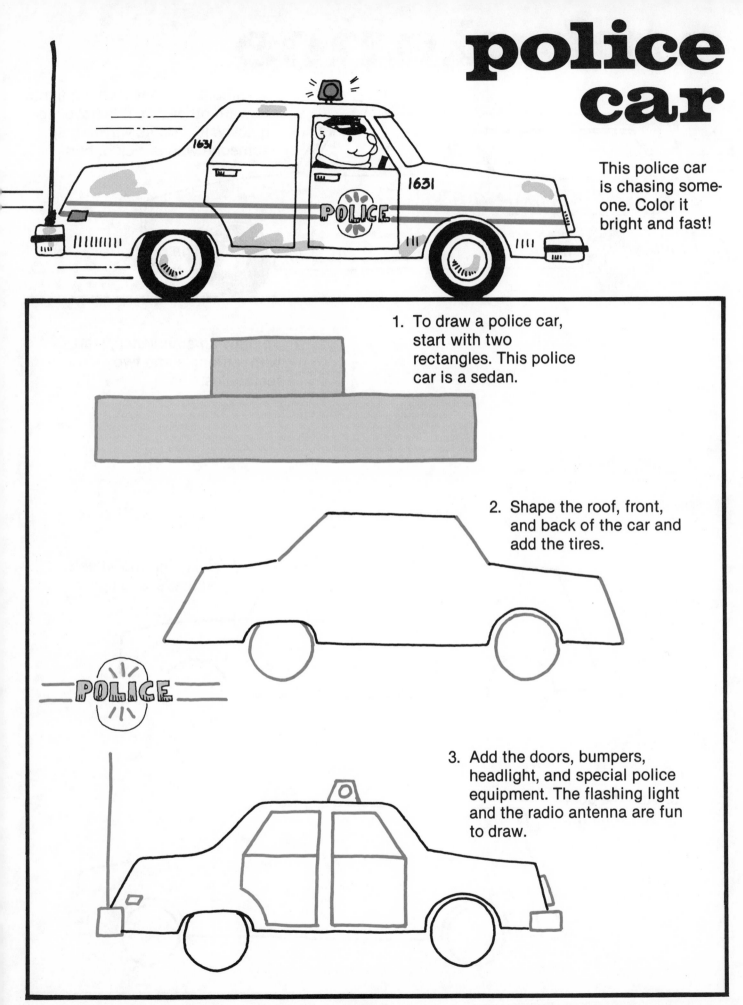

This police car is chasing someone. Color it bright and fast!

1. To draw a police car, start with two rectangles. This police car is a sedan.

2. Shape the roof, front, and back of the car and add the tires.

3. Add the doors, bumpers, headlight, and special police equipment. The flashing light and the radio antenna are fun to draw.

ambulance

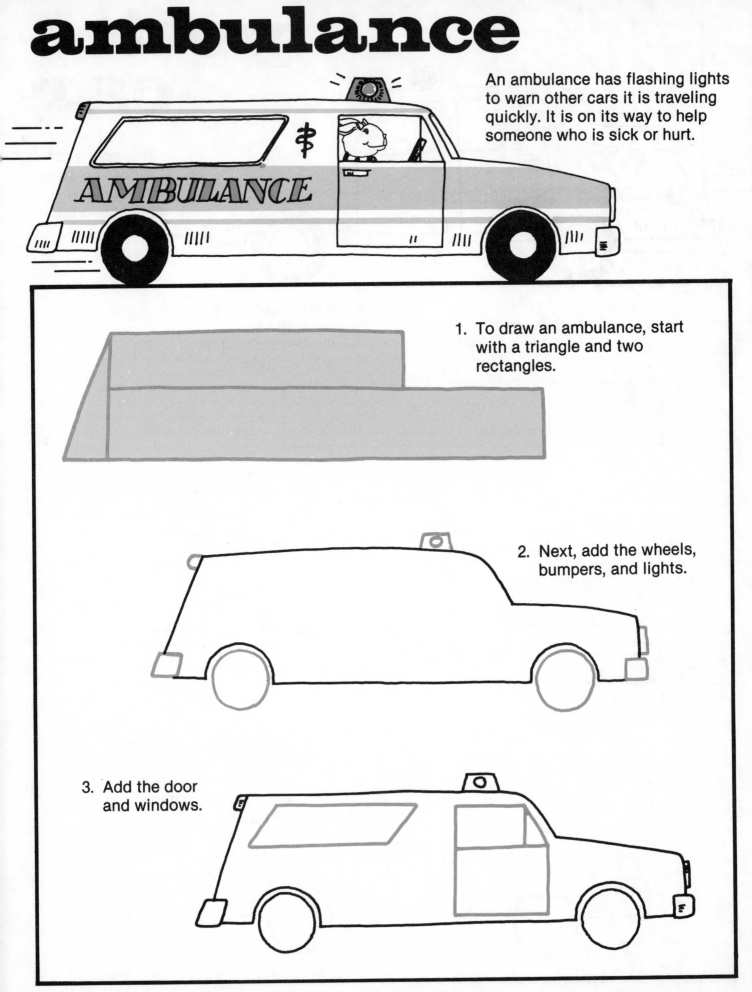

An ambulance has flashing lights to warn other cars it is traveling quickly. It is on its way to help someone who is sick or hurt.

1. To draw an ambulance, start with a triangle and two rectangles.

2. Next, add the wheels, bumpers, and lights.

3. Add the door and windows.

taxi cab

A taxi cab will take you to any part of town you want to go. Color it bright yellow.

1. To draw a taxi cab, start with two box shapes.

2. Now round off the boxes and add the tires.

3. Add the doors, bumpers, and lights.

Don't forget the mirror.

For the "checkerboard" design, draw four lines going from side to side. Then add lines going up and down. Now fill in every other box and there you have it.

dragster

Dragsters are funny-looking racing cars. The front wheels are like a bicycle's, and the rear wheels look like an airplane's. These brightly colored cars can go very fast.

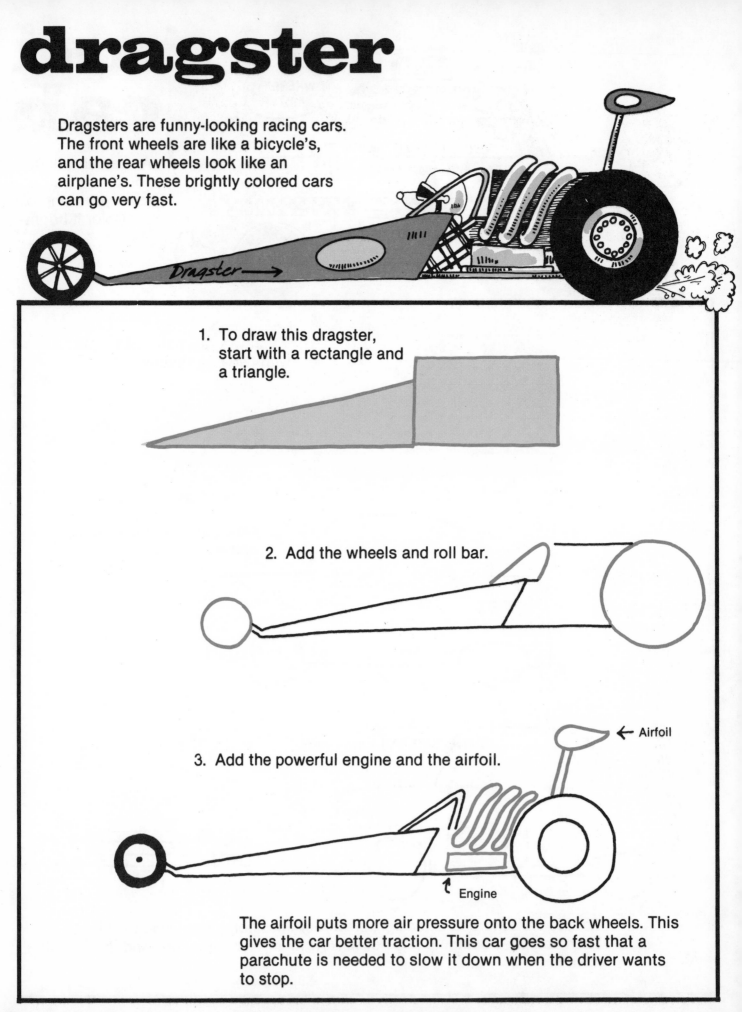

Dragster →

1. To draw this dragster, start with a rectangle and a triangle.

2. Add the wheels and roll bar.

3. Add the powerful engine and the airfoil.

← Airfoil

↑ Engine

The airfoil puts more air pressure onto the back wheels. This gives the car better traction. This car goes so fast that a parachute is needed to slow it down when the driver wants to stop.

This special racing car is known as a "Can-Am" car. It competes in many races in *Can*ada and *Am*erica.

racing car

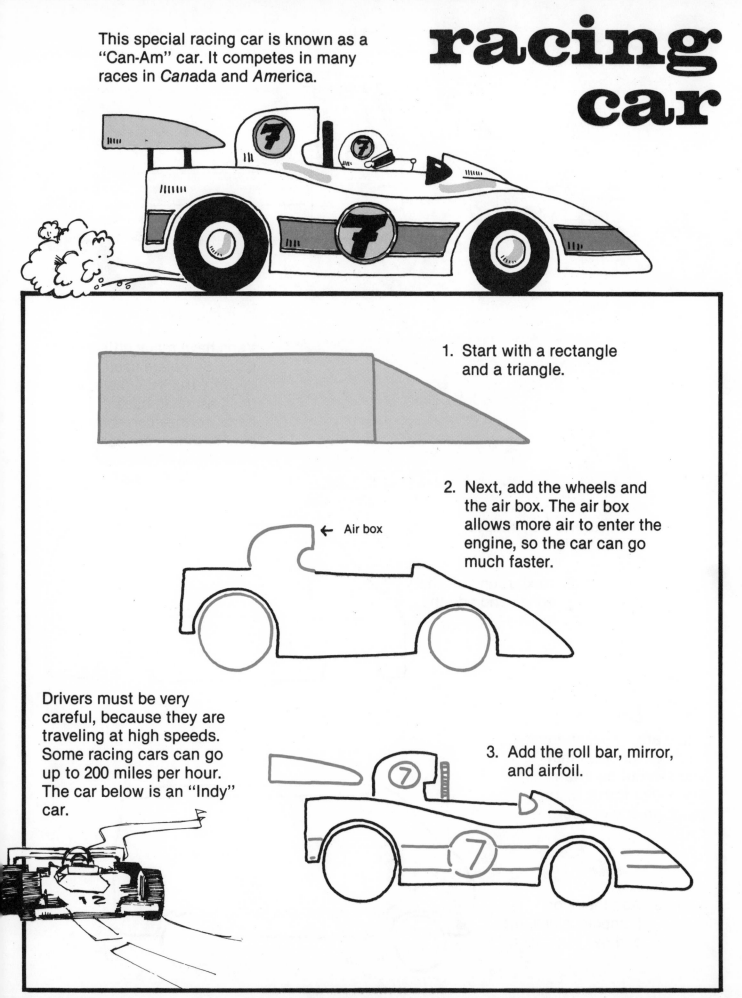

1. Start with a rectangle and a triangle.

2. Next, add the wheels and the air box. The air box allows more air to enter the engine, so the car can go much faster.

← Air box

Drivers must be very careful, because they are traveling at high speeds. Some racing cars can go up to 200 miles per hour. The car below is an "Indy" car.

3. Add the roll bar, mirror, and airfoil.

van

Vans have many different uses. Some are used as delivery trucks. Others are used as small buses, because they can seat more people than a car can. Some vans are even used as small "homes-on-wheels."

1. Start with two box shapes and a triangle.

2. Next, round off the edges and add the wheels.

There are many different kinds of windows that you can put on a van. Try one of these, or make up one of your own.

3. Add the door, bumpers, sidelights, and gas-tank door.

jeep

A jeep is a lightweight truck that was first widely used during World War II. This powerful little truck can go up steep hills and can even cross shallow streams.

1. To draw a jeep, start with three box shapes.

2. Connect the boxes and divide the jeep into two sections. (The tires will fit in the bottom section.)

Spare tire

3. Add the tires (don't forget the spare tire on the back). Draw a few lines to show the hood of the jeep.

Roll bar

4. Now add the roll bar, windshield, and seat.

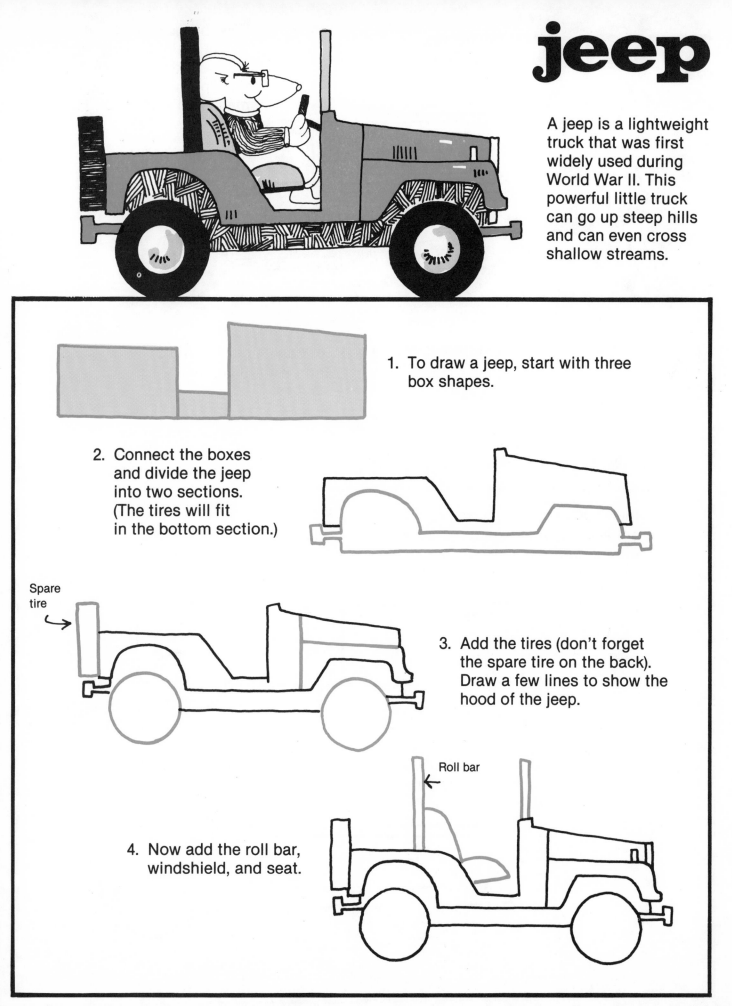

pickup

Pickup trucks are small trucks that can carry many different kinds of things. Pickup trucks can even be made into campers.

1. To draw a pickup truck, start with three box shapes.

2. Round off two of the boxes for the roof and the front end of the truck. Add the wheels, bumpers, and lights. Then add a long, thin rectangle to the side of the truck.

3. Add the door, windows, tailgate, and top light, and you have a pickup truck.

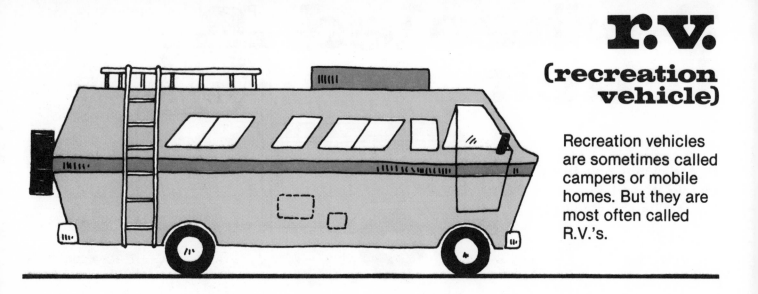

r.v.
(recreation vehicle)

Recreation vehicles are sometimes called campers or mobile homes. But they are most often called R.V.'s.

1. To draw this R.V., start with a large rectangle and two triangles.

2. Next, add the tires, windows, and door.

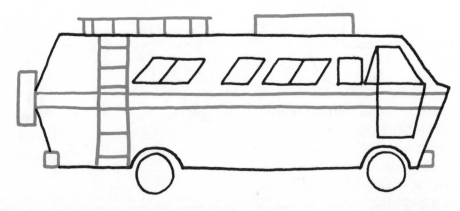

3. Add the ladder leading to the storage space, the bumpers, and spare tire.

3-wheeled truck

This truck has only three wheels. It can be used on city streets and sidewalks.

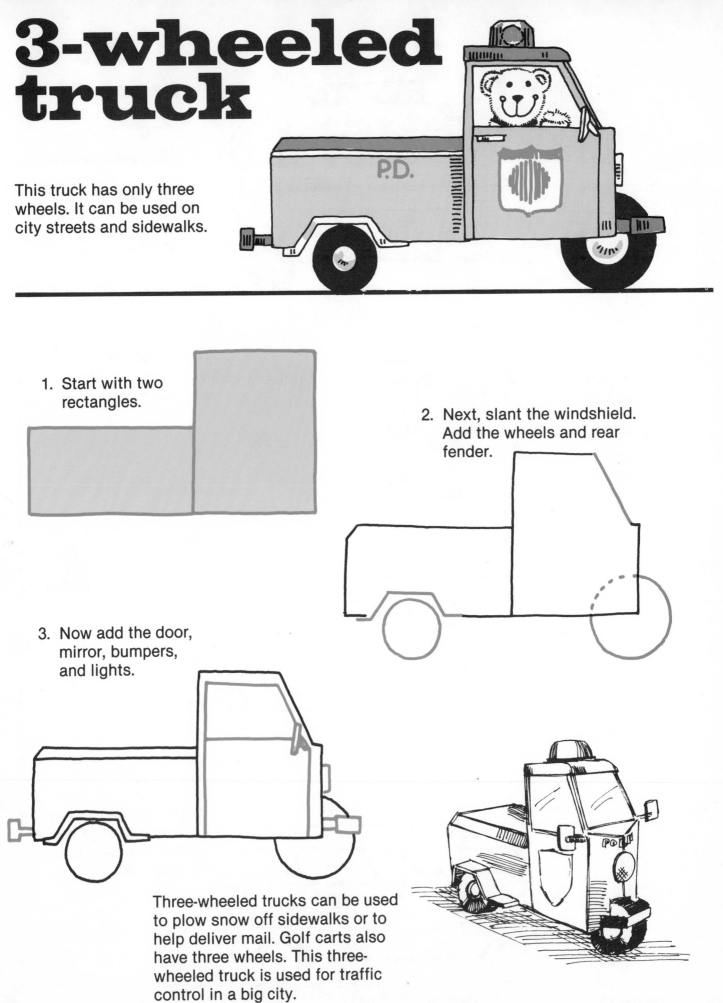

1. Start with two rectangles.

2. Next, slant the windshield. Add the wheels and rear fender.

3. Now add the door, mirror, bumpers, and lights.

Three-wheeled trucks can be used to plow snow off sidewalks or to help deliver mail. Golf carts also have three wheels. This three-wheeled truck is used for traffic control in a big city.

A cab is the front part of a very big truck. The powerful engine is in the cab, and this is what pulls the weight of the truck.

10-4 GOOD BUDDY

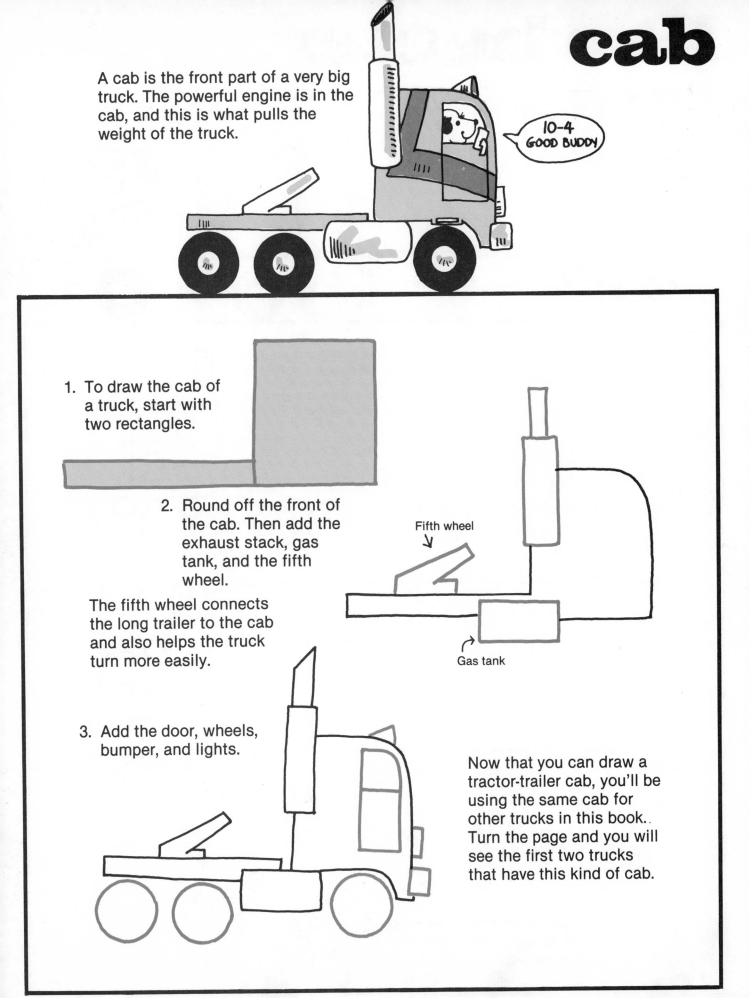

1. To draw the cab of a truck, start with two rectangles.

2. Round off the front of the cab. Then add the exhaust stack, gas tank, and the fifth wheel.

The fifth wheel connects the long trailer to the cab and also helps the truck turn more easily.

Fifth wheel

Gas tank

3. Add the door, wheels, bumper, and lights.

Now that you can draw a tractor-trailer cab, you'll be using the same cab for other trucks in this book. Turn the page and you will see the first two trucks that have this kind of cab.

18-wheeler

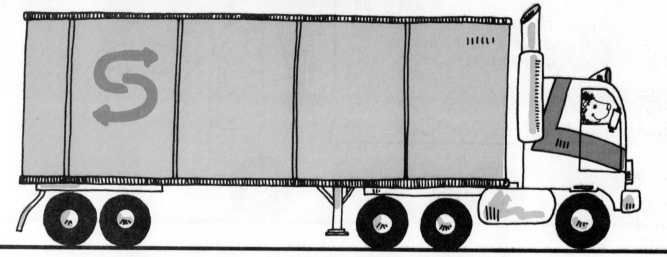

1. Now that you know how to draw the cab, an 18-wheeler is easy!
Start with a large rectangle.

2. Now add the rear tires, the support, and lines for the panels of the truck.

This truck has 18 wheels. This is how they are arranged.

A low-bed truck can carry large pieces of equipment on its open, flat back. This one's carrying a bulldozer.

low bed

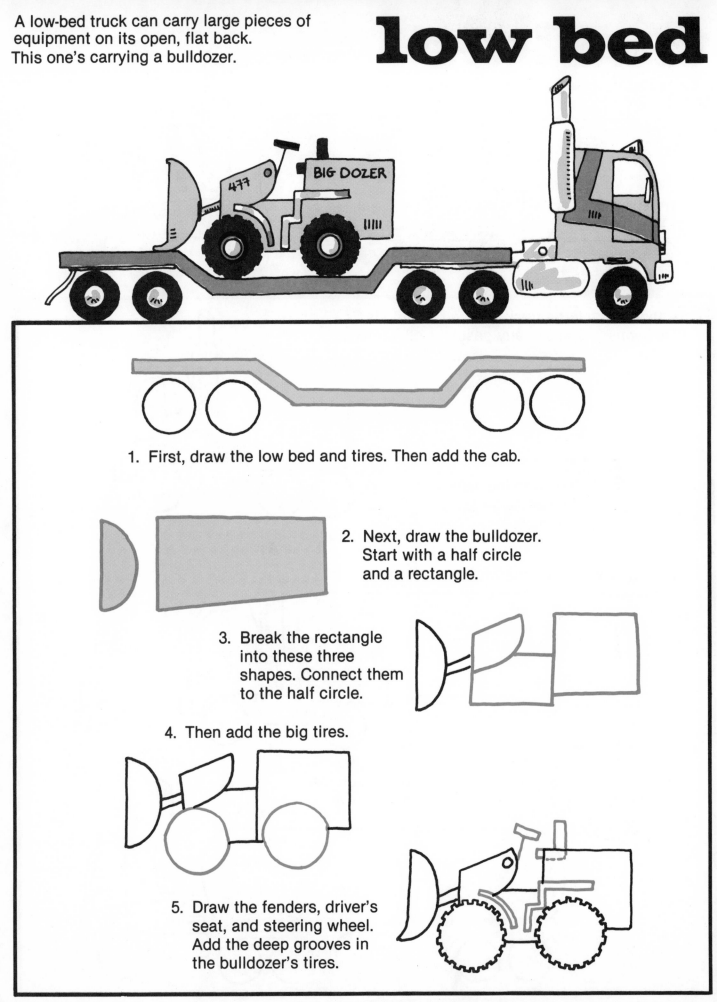

1. First, draw the low bed and tires. Then add the cab.

2. Next, draw the bulldozer. Start with a half circle and a rectangle.

3. Break the rectangle into these three shapes. Connect them to the half circle.

4. Then add the big tires.

5. Draw the fenders, driver's seat, and steering wheel. Add the deep grooves in the bulldozer's tires.

tanker

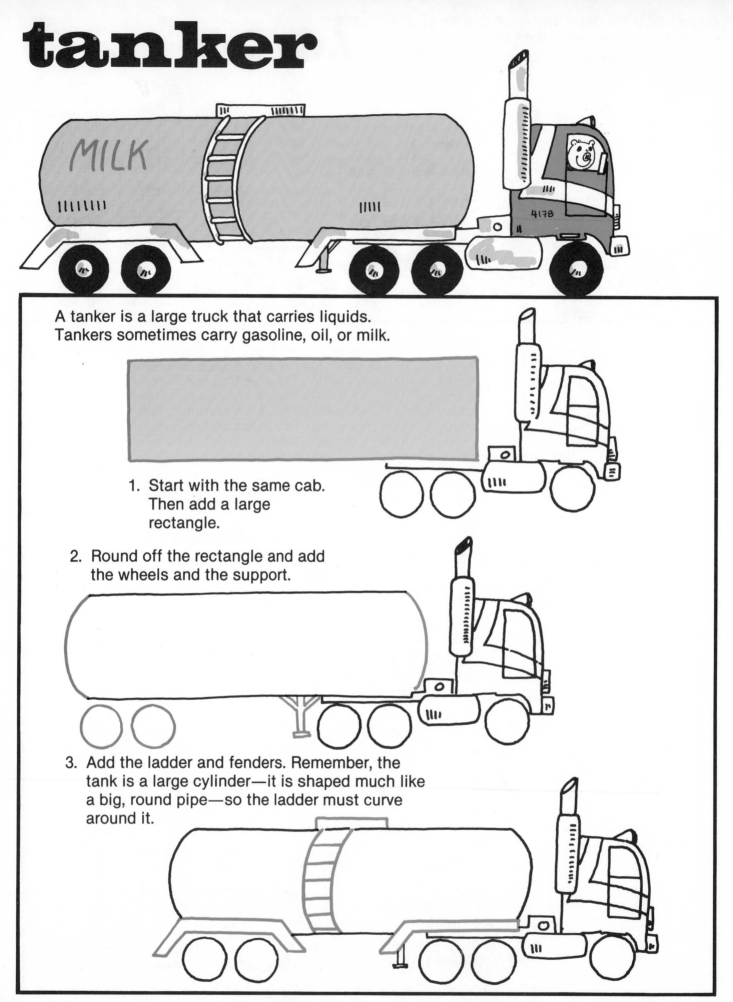

A tanker is a large truck that carries liquids.
Tankers sometimes carry gasoline, oil, or milk.

1. Start with the same cab.
   Then add a large
   rectangle.

2. Round off the rectangle and add
   the wheels and the support.

3. Add the ladder and fenders. Remember, the
   tank is a large cylinder—it is shaped much like
   a big, round pipe—so the ladder must curve
   around it.

auto carrier

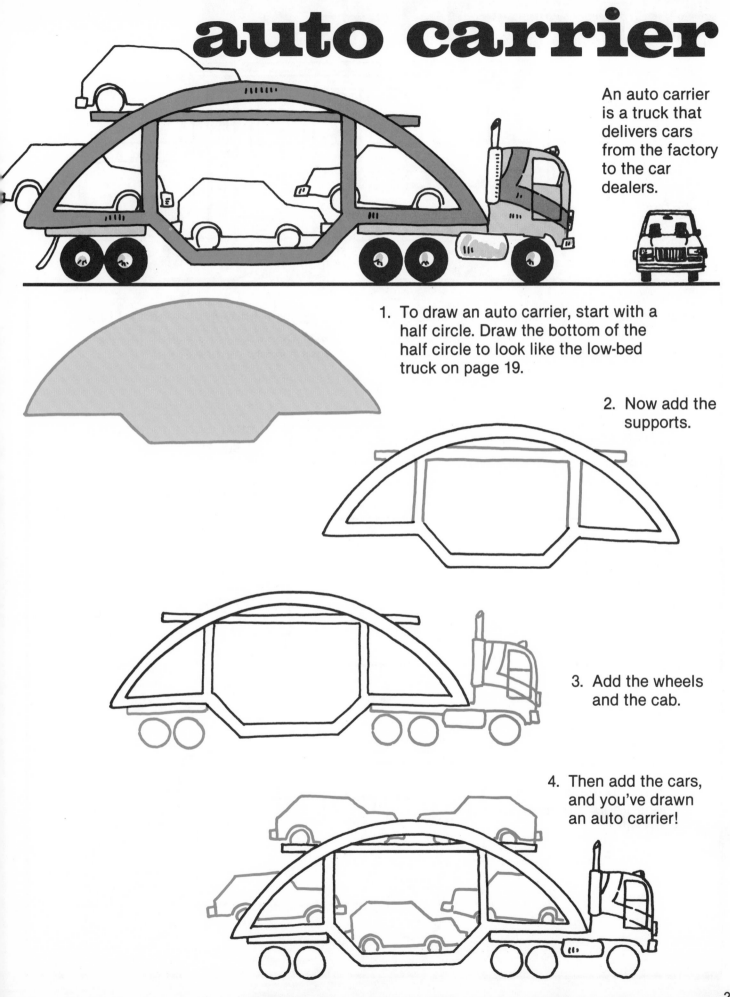

An auto carrier is a truck that delivers cars from the factory to the car dealers.

1. To draw an auto carrier, start with a half circle. Draw the bottom of the half circle to look like the low-bed truck on page 19.

2. Now add the supports.

3. Add the wheels and the cab.

4. Then add the cars, and you've drawn an auto carrier!

school bus

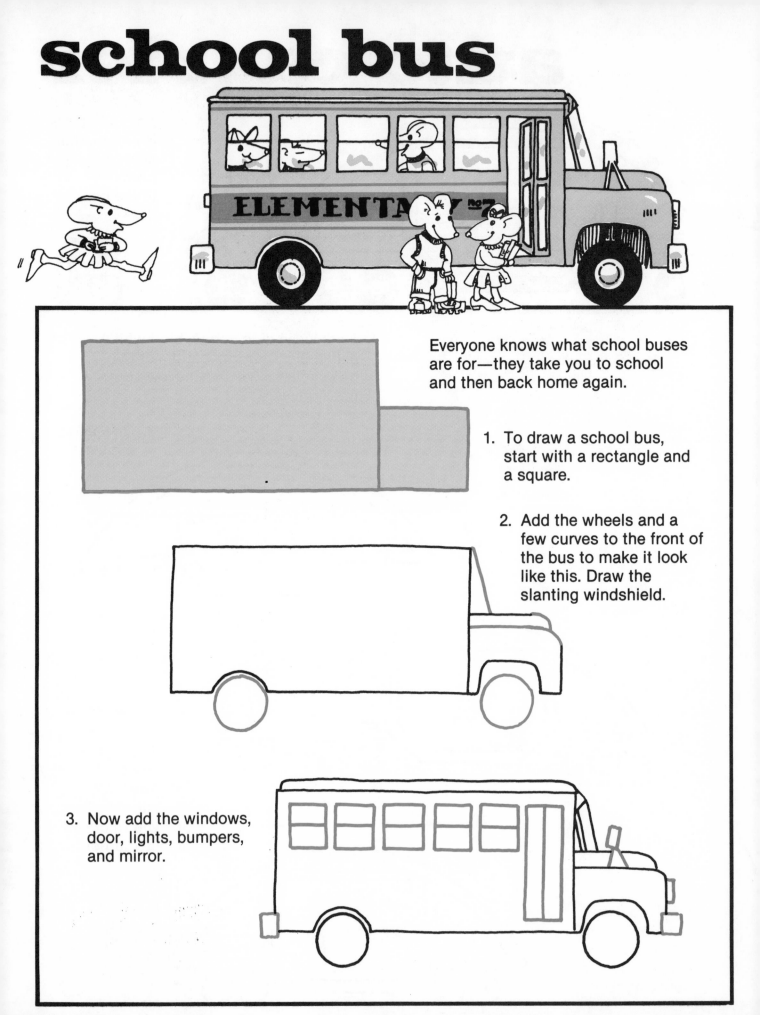

Everyone knows what school buses are for—they take you to school and then back home again.

1. To draw a school bus, start with a rectangle and a square.

2. Add the wheels and a few curves to the front of the bus to make it look like this. Draw the slanting windshield.

3. Now add the windows, door, lights, bumpers, and mirror.

fire engine

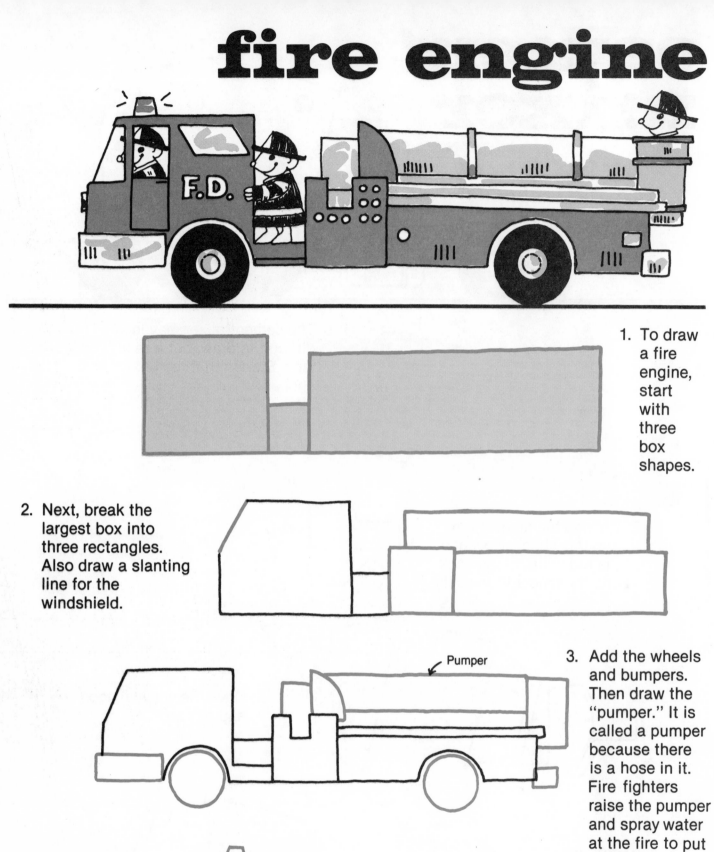

1. To draw a fire engine, start with three box shapes.

2. Next, break the largest box into three rectangles. Also draw a slanting line for the windshield.

Pumper

3. Add the wheels and bumpers. Then draw the "pumper." It is called a pumper because there is a hose in it. Fire fighters raise the pumper and spray water at the fire to put it out.

4. Look carefully at all the details before you draw them. Don't forget the door, windows, and flashing light.

cement mixer

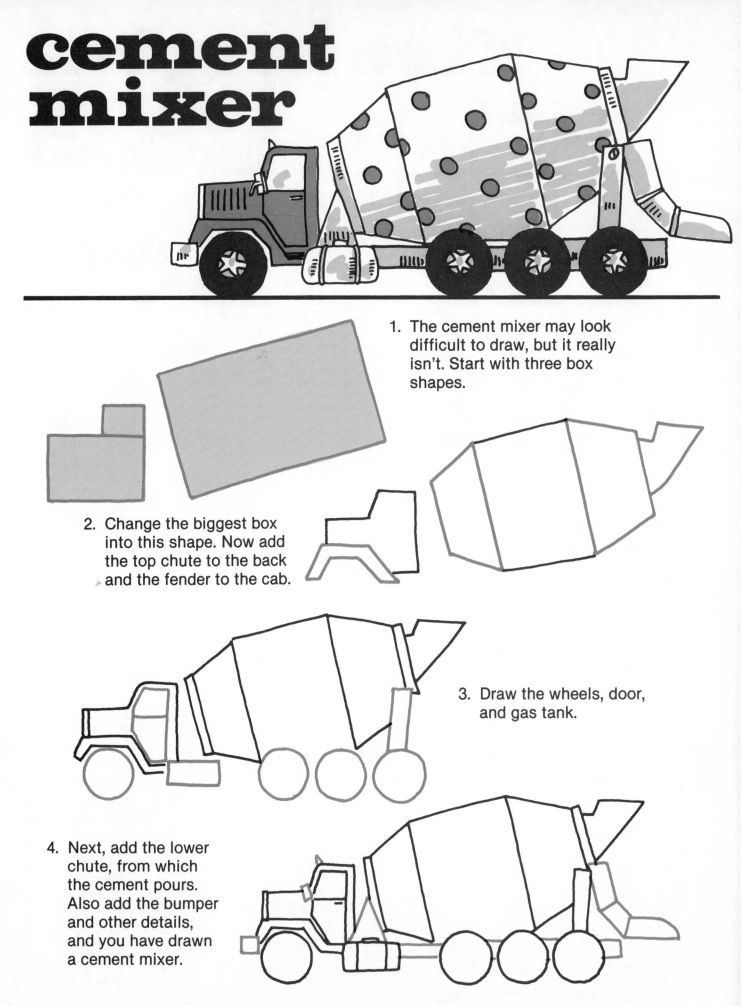

1. The cement mixer may look difficult to draw, but it really isn't. Start with three box shapes.

2. Change the biggest box into this shape. Now add the top chute to the back and the fender to the cab.

3. Draw the wheels, door, and gas tank.

4. Next, add the lower chute, from which the cement pours. Also add the bumper and other details, and you have drawn a cement mixer.

dump truck

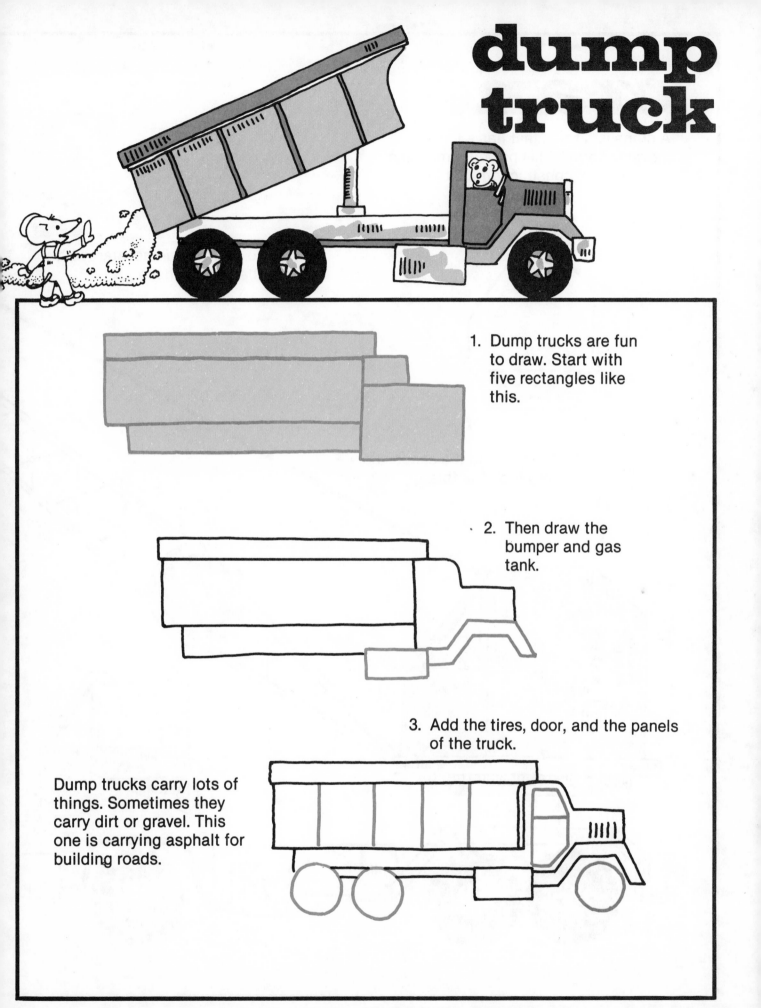

1. Dump trucks are fun to draw. Start with five rectangles like this.

2. Then draw the bumper and gas tank.

3. Add the tires, door, and the panels of the truck.

Dump trucks carry lots of things. Sometimes they carry dirt or gravel. This one is carrying asphalt for building roads.

crane

A crane is a truck that has a long, movable "arm." This powerful machine can do many construction jobs.

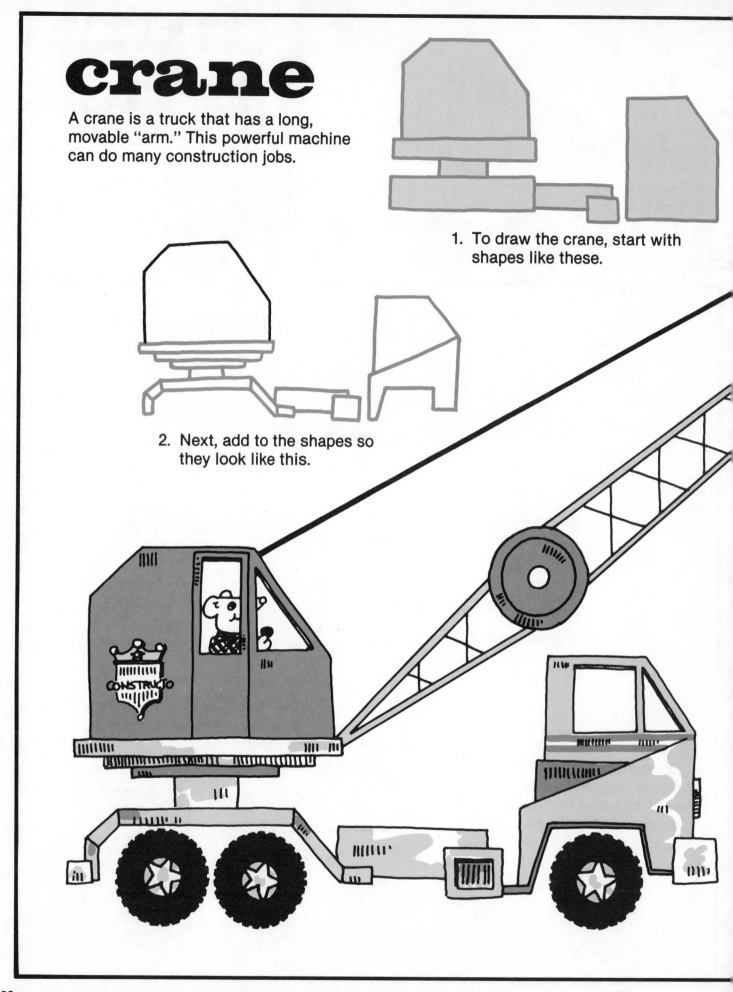

1. To draw the crane, start with shapes like these.

2. Next, add to the shapes so they look like this.

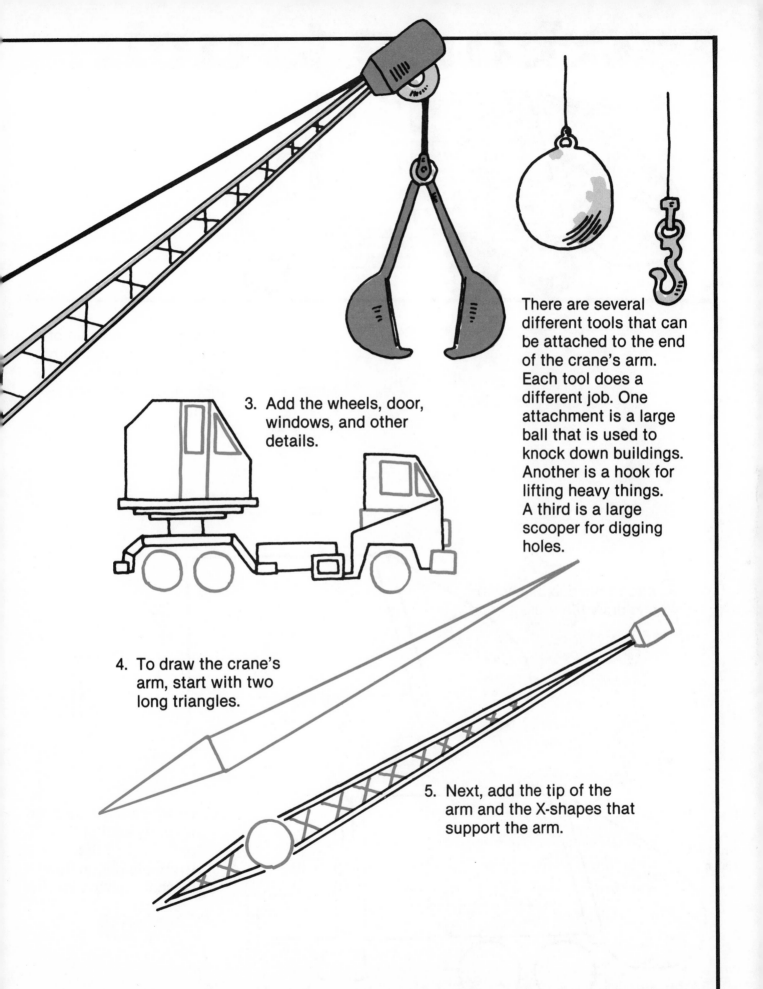

3. Add the wheels, door, windows, and other details.

There are several different tools that can be attached to the end of the crane's arm. Each tool does a different job. One attachment is a large ball that is used to knock down buildings. Another is a hook for lifting heavy things. A third is a large scooper for digging holes.

4. To draw the crane's arm, start with two long triangles.

5. Next, add the tip of the arm and the X-shapes that support the arm.

garbage truck

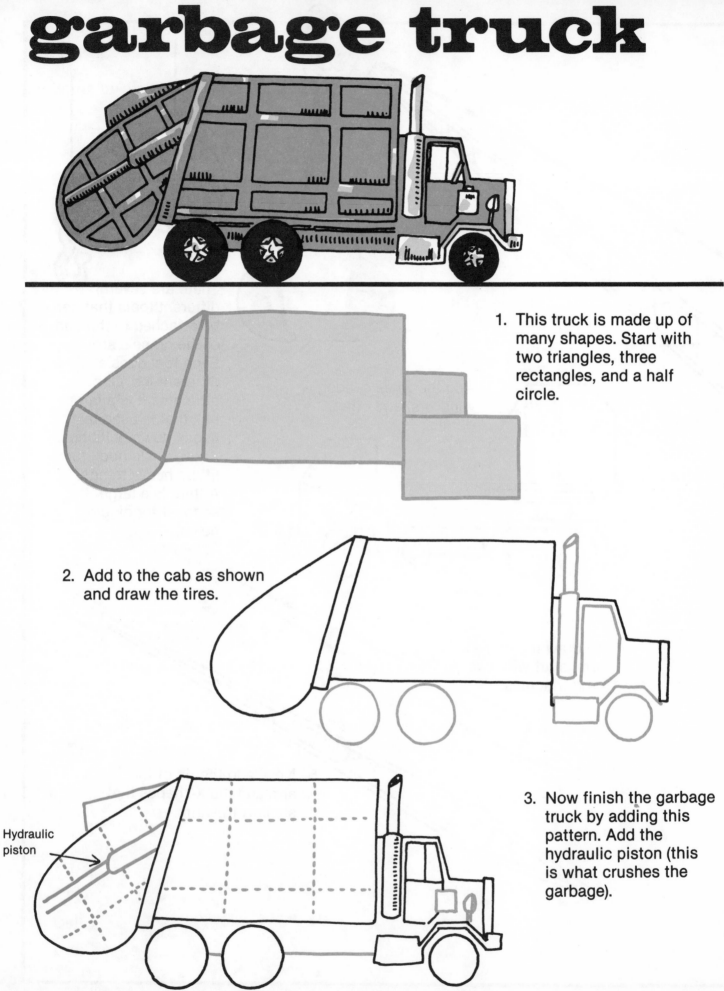

1. This truck is made up of many shapes. Start with two triangles, three rectangles, and a half circle.

2. Add to the cab as shown and draw the tires.

3. Now finish the garbage truck by adding this pattern. Add the hydraulic piston (this is what crushes the garbage).

Hydraulic piston

tow truck

A tow truck looks like a pickup truck. Its special job is to help other cars and trucks when they are broken down, by towing them to a garage for repairs.

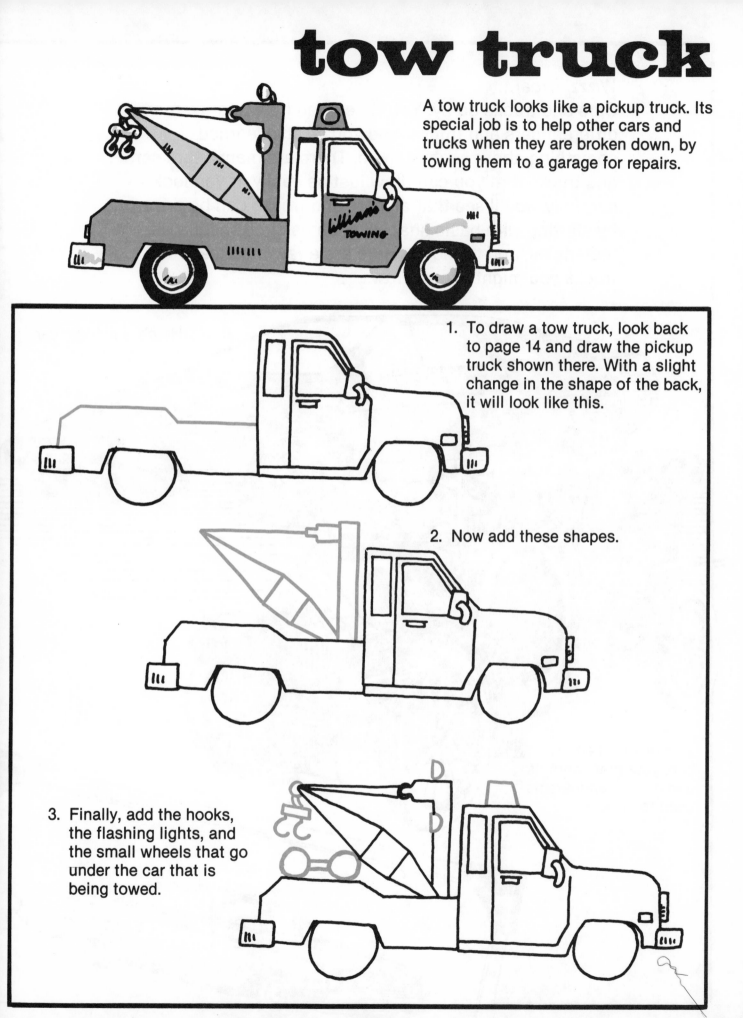

1. To draw a tow truck, look back to page 14 and draw the pickup truck shown there. With a slight change in the shape of the back, it will look like this.

2. Now add these shapes.

3. Finally, add the hooks, the flashing lights, and the small wheels that go under the car that is being towed.

Wizzz, rrroar...
Cars and trucks go by. You've learned how to draw many different cars and trucks, and you've also learned something about each of them. There are many more cars and trucks that you can draw just as easily. If you look carefully, you'll see that all cars and trucks can be drawn by starting with basic shapes, such as circles, squares, rectangles, and triangles. Here are a few more cars and trucks you might like to draw.

Here's a modern car.

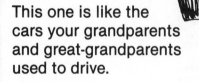

This one is like the cars your grandparents and great-grandparents used to drive.

Big rigs like this one move many products across the country.

Times have changed—just compare an 18-wheeler to this horse-drawn ice truck of many years ago!